For information, please contact SSU Publications, 559-706-4081

Every effort has been made to ensure the accuracy and completeness of information contained in this book. We assume no responsibility for errors, inaccuracies, omissions, or any inconsistency herein. Any slights of people, places, or organizations are unintentional.

ISBN 0-9725914-3-5

For information, please contact SSU Publications, 559-706-4081.

This book is dedicated to our children

Jon Frederick Morse, Jr.

Jason Allen Morse

Jennifer Marie Payne

When we realized we were going to become parents, we vowed to be the best parents we could possibly be. This doesn't mean that we were perfect parents it just means we did the best we could. Our children were our testing ground. We want to thank them profusely for putting up with all the mistakes we made as we worked to understand children and young people and what was needed for them to be healthy, well adjusted adults who would become a contributing force in our world. Despite the fact that they were our experimental laboratory, we are very fortunate that they have far exceeded our expectations.

"It is better to light a candle than to curse the darkness"

Ancient Chinese Proverb

LIGHT A CANDLE OR CURSE THE DARKNESS

HOW TO CONNECT WITH AMERICA'S YOUTH

Jon F. Morse, Sr., M.A.

Mary A. Morse, M.S.

SSU Publications

CHOOSING
(In my life I am the chooser)

Do I say "Look what life is doing to me"? or

Do I say "Look what I am doing to life"?

There is power in choosing.

There is special power in knowing I am the chooser at every moment in every situation. Even when I do not take action. Even when I do not make a decision. I am choosing to not decide. I am choosing to not take action.

At every moment I choose who I keep company with- or not to keep company.

I choose what I learn or not to learn anything

I choose how I spend my time-including choosing to not choose.

In life I choose my mentors- or not to have a mentor, not to admire and emulate anybody, not to ask for help.

When I go out the door, I turn right or left, or go straight ahead. The path I take can influence my whole life. I can even choose not to go out at all.

Most importantly, I choose which ideas, actions, foods, drinks, substances I say "no" to and which I say "yes" to.

I teach myself a thousand times a day to make brilliant decisions- or not.

Sami Sunchild/Author
Red Victorian Peace Center
1665 Haight Street
San Francisco, CA 94117
415-864-1978

P.S.   CHOOSERS HAVE NO ADDICTIONS
ADDICTS HAVE NO CHOICES

Table of Contents

ACKNOWLEDGEMENTS

There have been many individuals that have been instrumental in getting this book on the shelf. We have done our best to acknowledge each and everyone. If by chance someone has been omitted, it is certainly not intentional.

We would like to thank the following:

Cort Elgar who for the past 28 years has been an integral part of our family. He has been encouraging us for the past two years to complete this book.

Mary's sister, Phyllis Jackson, who did a great job of editing for grammatical errors that have kept this book from becoming a comedy of errors.

Sami Sunchild for the use of her poem "Choosing" that has been instrumental in conveying the message of choice in my trainings throughout California.

Dr. William Glasser and his wife Carleen who have been available to answer the many questions that have brought this project to completion.

Tom Kellner who inspired the title for the book and wrote the forward.

Nasreen McMullen for her excellent work in designing the cover.

A special thank you to our oldest son Jon who has spent many hours preparing the book for printing and also for his photography work for the cover.

Last but certainly not least are the individuals who have read and given us invaluable feedback. Our thanks go to these very important people in our lives: Jason Morse, Beth Bajuk, Jennifer Payne, Michael Payne, Cort Elgar, Sandra Brawner, Tom Kellner, Aleta Warner, Dr. William Glasser, Carleen Glasser, Connie Clendenon.

ABOUT THE AUTHORS

Jon Frederick Morse, Sr. M.A.
Mary Annah Morse, M.S.

We would like to welcome you and give you a little background information. We were married in 1965 when Jon was 19 and Mary was 18 years of age. Shortly after we were married we became the leaders of the youth group at the church where we were members. So we can honestly say we have been working with teens since we were teenagers.

Jon has a Bachelor of Arts Degree in Psychology and a Master of Arts Degree in Counseling, a Teaching Credential and is a Master Practitioner in the field of Neuro Linguistic Programming. He has worked in the fields of probation, mental health, youth ministry, coaching, teaching and counseling. During the last four years Jon has facilitated hundreds of trainings with schools, corrections departments, transportation departments, and corporate businesses locally in the San Joaquin Valley and throughout California. He is currently working as Executive Director to develop a charter school for high school students in Fresno. Jon has aligned himself with Big Picture Schools, Inc., a non-profit organization in California that shares a common vision for assisting students in their academic endeavors.

Mary has a Bachelor of Arts Degree in Family Studies, a Master of Science Degree in Counseling and is a Master Practitioner in the field of Neuro Linguistic Programming. She worked behind the scenes raising their three children, Jon, Jr., Jason and Jennifer and giving Jon the emotional support he needed to continue to learn and grow and do everything in his power to assist young people through their incredible journey to adulthood.

Jon has had the field experience and since he has shared these experiences through the years with Mary, and received valuable feedback, she has been an integral part of this process. Her writing skills have also made this book possible. We have worked together to share with you the experiences and successes we have shared over the years.

We have learned so much over the past 42 years and have had so many successes we feel we need to share what we have learned with as many people as possible. We cannot reach everyone, but we can assist and encourage others to join with us to do our best to turn the tide as we meet the emotional needs of our youth today.

FORWARD

In this book, Jon Morse has provided us with ideas for listening to, caring for, and helping others. By following his step-by-step techniques, we can help those who have made unwise choices. Jon's approach enables those who have made unwise choices to turn their lives around. This is accomplished by discovering that the only answer to misery and despair comes from within and from making new and better choices. In the making of new choices, people will find a pathway toward personal power and fulfillment. These ideas and practices come from a lifelong search on Jon's part for ways to help people he cares about, including his former students and now his present clients. Jon's techniques have been rapidly enhanced by the influence of Dr. William Glasser's ideas of choice theory. Jon has enthusiastically spent many hours in training with Dr. Glasser's materials and is interweaving Dr. Glasser's ideas with his own.

Jon is a REAL person who cares about life and people. It is clear that he is an effective teacher and communicator. He understands the use of words and ideas. Words, in fact, are his tools. Ideas are his pathway of life. People are his object of concern.

In this short book, we have a step-by-step road map designed to show us how to help people help themselves. Don't just read this book. Instead, use it as a standard to reach out, to listen, to communicate, and to provide ideas for choices that will help move people to an awareness that they are in charge of their lives. That the good life comes from within. That each individual chooses the quality of his or her own life.

Jon is as real as he seems to be in his book and is an inspiration as a friend and fellow educator. He is a leader! One who can effectively teach others how to create brighter futures for themselves.

> Thomas L. Kellner
> Retired Principal, Independence High School
> Planning Commissioner, District 1, Madera County

PREFACE

This book has been a project that has been inspired out of a need to share some concepts that Jon has created while working with the young people who have had trouble in the past making connections with significant adults in their lives. All around us we hear people talking about how our teenagers here in America are so bad and how much trouble they cause. If there is a problem, it is usually caused by some teenager somewhere.

Jon was traveling to Los Angeles with a friend, Tom Kellner. Tom had read the manuscript and asked if we had come up with a title for the book. Jon confided that we had really been struggling with a title that would really grab people's attention and let them know what they could do to help our young people. He suggested an old Chinese Proverb, "Better to light a candle than to curse the darkness". Jon repeated it over and over again and he had an inexpressible feeling of congruency between the proverb and the message we were trying to convey.

"Light a Candle or Curse the Darkness" gives us all a choice. We can either sit back and complain about our youth and the trouble they are causing or we can light a candle that will lead them toward individuals who really want to make a connection and who are willing to help them through some of the most difficult years they will experience.

We challenge each of you who read this book to light a candle with us and then share this book with others who feel that the young people in America need a light to follow so that they can escape from the darkness of not being connected with significant adults in their lives.

Thank you Tom for your insight and desire to see this book come to fruition. Your friendship and support is greatly appreciated.

INTRODUCTION

"Before anyone can expect to have an impact and see any significant progress with teens who are having social, academic or behavioral problems, it is critical to establish an emotional connection."

In the fictional movie "The Wizard of Oz, four individuals, Dorothy, the Lion, the Tin Man and the Scarecrow, happen to meet and become a quartet of new friends traveling the yellow brick road to see the Wizard. Each of the characters in this story had a problem that needed to be solved. They each believed that by traveling to the city of Oz and making their requests known to the Wizard he would be able to grant them their specific wish. In the end, they realized the Wizard was just an ordinary man who understood what they needed and helped them to discover that the answers they were looking for resided within themselves and could be garnered by changing the way they thought about themselves.

In our world today many young people are just like these fictional characters before they met the Wizard. Their lives are troubled and they always place blame on external factors for their difficulties. These young people, for whatever reason, have not encountered significant individuals who possess the belief in them and the ability to help them realize their full potential. What they really need is someone to help them realize that remaining a victim is a personal choice. In actuality, within their minds, they have all the resources they need to find the solutions to their difficulties in life.

All around the world, troubled teens face authority figures. Most of the time this happens, not because they have chosen to seek help like Dorothy and her friends, but because of some type of negative behavior. Authority figures may include; parents, teachers, principals, coaches, employers and even law enforcement, corrections and probation officers. These individuals are placed in a position where they must decide what action to take regarding behaviors such as tardiness, lying, stealing, drug use, alcohol abuse, violence, etc.

In what way can these authority figures relate to young people? How can they help them realize they are in control of the consequences for their actions? These are not easy questions. Typically most ideas or plans of action call for some kind of punishment that will "magically" cause these teenagers to begin to behave in a responsible manner. Dr. William Glasser refers to this prevailing societal belief as "the psychology of external control". This belief is used in our homes, in the courts, in our schools and other organizations because these methods have been relied upon and passed down for generations. External control takes place when we force our views upon another person and believe that what is right for us is right for them. Our institutions spend large sums of money to implement external control strategies, hoping they will correct the difficult people they have to face every day. It is obvious by the increased building of prisons and our increasing crime rate that this type of approach is not working. In fact, our young people react even more strongly to a "heavy handed" approach that communicates "you will do it my way or else!"

It is extremely important for all of us to understand that all behavior is a choice and it will move us toward pleasure and away from pain. Many times the negative behaviors we see teens participating in such as drugs, alcohol, sex, thrill seeking activities, etc., are giving them pleasure. They make these choices because it gives them a sense of control and power. The more external control is forced upon them the more they move toward establishing their own internal control. The pleasure they get from these behaviors is more satisfying than anything else they can experience at home or at school. In order for these teenagers to make a paradigm shift to responsible choices and behavior, they must see the relationship between their decisions and the effects they are getting in their lives.

Before anyone can expect to have an impact and see any significant progress with teens who are having social, academic or behavioral problems, it is critical to establish an emotional connection. I have found that in most cases, when we take the time to get to know these young people and make that connection in a one-on-one situation, the changes in future behaviors can be very significant.

This process can be used by any one of you who are reading this book. It is very simple. However, there is one secret you must know before you begin the process of establishing a relationship. The secret is that you must genuinely care about the individual. What you believe about troubled youth and the expectations you have for them will be the main component that enables a young person to desire a change in their lives. They must feel the passion and unconditional regard you have for them. Without this element you will only be going through the motions. They will walk away from you feeling that you are just like all the other authority figures in their lives. Your beliefs about young people determine what action you will take and the affect it will have on their lives.

Working with teens can be a very rewarding experience when using the tools that are most effective. I want to give you a step by step methodological system that I have found to be effective time after time with troubled teenagers. I am sure this approach will give you the enjoyment and satisfaction I have experienced while working with these young people.

A
GUIDED
TOUR

*"Kids don't care how much you know
until they know how much you care"*

I am going to be taking you on a very specific guided tour of a typical intervention session with a troubled teenager. This teenager had been referred to me because he had been acting out, skipping school, failing his classes, etc. The young people I have worked with come in all varieties of sizes, shapes and mental capacities. The one common ground they all share is their decision making strategies. These strategies are causing conflicts for themselves and their families. It is very typical that they are in denial about their difficulties and when confronted about their actions assume a victims role and blame everyone and everything in their environment for their difficulties. This section will be a very specific and definitive recall of a typical 30 minute session with a teenager and his mother. You will notice the importance I place on having the young person learn to be very specific when giving his answers. I let him know that I will be completely honest with him, therefore I expect him to be completely honest with me. The following example is a typical interview with a troubled young man we will call Jeff.

Jeff and his mom are waiting for me on the second floor of

our office complex. As I enter the upstairs office, I greet Jeff and his mother with a warm smile and handshake.

"Jeff, I am really glad to meet you. I have really been looking forward to this meeting."

After the initial greeting I invite them to join me in the conference room for our session together. I have Jeff and his mother sit across from me so they can both see the chalk board which is directly behind me. After they sit down, I thank them for coming. I let them know I am very excited to have the opportunity to meet them both. I tell Jeff's mother she can listen in while we are talking. During the session, I make it a point to use Jeff's name quite often. I have also found it to be extremely important to repeat back to the student his responses to me, to ensure that I truly understand what he or she is conveying to me. I give him my total undivided attention. I let him know he is a very important person and the only thing that matters in the next 30 minutes is what takes place between the two of us. Then as I speak I look directly at Jeff.

"Jeff, the next 30 minutes you will be spending with me will be quite different from anything you have previously experienced. I am looking for young people who really want to do something different and be successful. So, by the time we finish this session together, you will be able to be completely honest with me and tell me if this program is what you're looking for. Does that make sense?"

"Yeah, it does."

"Great, then let's get started. Jeff, tell me a little bit about your elementary school years, kindergarten through sixth grade."

"My elementary school years were okay."

"Jeff, could you give me more specific information like what your grades were like?"

"Well, I mostly got A's, B's and C's."

"Great, what was your favorite subject?"

"I really liked art and P.E."

"So Jeff, tell me, how did you get along with your teachers and classmates in elementary school?"

"Pretty good. I never really got into any kind of trouble."

"So, from what you've told me so far, we could say that your elementary school years were happy ones, you got pretty good grades and you got along with your teachers and classmates. Is that correct?"

"Yeah, that's right."

"Jeff, would you please describe what it was like for you when you started attending junior high or middle school."

"I started junior high when I was about 13. It was really different. I didn't have just one teacher like I used to have. I had a different teacher for each class and I only had one or two of my friends in a couple of classes. It was so big that I hardly got to see any of my friends."

"Would you say this was a good experience or a bad one?"

"Well, it was really different. I didn't know too many people and I just didn't feel like I fit in. I guess it really wasn't a very good time for me."

"Jeff, tell me what your grades were like."

"Well, I started off pretty good but then they started going down pretty fast. My teachers really started bugging me and my parents weren't very happy with my report card."

"Anything else?"

"I started having trouble with some of the other kids. I got into a couple of fights and got expelled from school for a few days."

"Then what happened?"

"My grades got worse and I just didn't want to go to school any more. I would fake like I was sick or I would pretend to go to school and ditch with some of my friends who hated school too."

"So, how were your grades at the end of the semester?"

"Not very good."

Jeff, could you be more specific? What do you mean by not very good?"

"Well, I think I got mostly D's and F's, except for art and of course, P.E."

"How did everything go for you during your eighth grade year?

"Worse!"

"What do you mean it got worse?"

"I wasn't doing well and no one seemed to care so I decided I wasn't going to go to school. So, me and some of my friends would ditch. We made our parents think we were in school but we just ditched. We got away with it for a long time but eventually they caught us."

"So what happened after they caught up with you and your friends?"

"I got put on probation. I have a probation officer that checks up on me to see that I am attending school every day. I still don't like school and I don't want to be here."

"I can see you are being honest with me. I really appreciate that. So Jeff, what is going to happen if you continue to do what you are currently doing?"

"I'm not sure. I think they're going to kick me out of this school. I'll probably have to go somewhere else."

"So, is that what you want?"

"Not really, my friends are here and I wouldn't know anyone at those other schools."

"So, let me get this straight. You really want to stay at this school because your close friends all attend here, but your grades are all F's and your counselor and the administrators are wanting to kick you out because you are not passing any of your classes. Is that right?"

"Yeah, I guess."

"Jeff, thank you for being honest with me about everything."

Now, because Jeff has been honest with me about his feelings and behaviors I know the time is right to begin helping him to see the relationship between his decisions and the consequences he is now experiencing in his life. So, I go for it!

I start by tossing a piece of chalk up into the air and catching it. I do this repeatedly, at least five or six times. Instinctively, Jeff begins to follow the chalk with his eyes.

"Jeff, why does the piece of chalk not stay up in the air?"

"Well, I guess because of gravity."

"So Jeff, is gravity real or not?"

"I guess it's real."

"Right, we call gravity a law or principle of the universe. What would happen if one of your friends told you he was going to jump from this second floor over to the building across the courtyard?"

"I'd try to stop him!"

"Why?"

"Because he would get hurt or killed!"

"Right. I knew you were pretty smart. So, if you really cared about your friend you would try to stop him from jumping."

"Yeah!"

"Would there be another way to get to the other building without trying to jump?"

"Sure, he could walk down the stairs and get a ladder to get to the top of the other building or climb the stairs inside if there were any."

"Right! He could make another choice. These new choices, would they be good choices or bad ones?"

"Good ones."

"Why?"

"He could get where he wanted to go without getting hurt or killing himself."

"Good job Jeff. Now let's review. We have established that gravity is a law, it is real and if anyone goes against the law of gravity some serious problems like injury or death could be a result of that decision. Is that right?"

"Yeah."

"Jeff, let me introduce you to another law that is even more powerful than the law of gravity and is either working for us or against us because of the decisions and choices we make. I call this law the "law of cause and effect" or "sowing and reaping". This law states that as a result of whatever I choose to do or not do I will receive some kind of positive or negative consequence or reward. So, when I make a good decision I get good results. When I make a bad decision, I get bad results. Good in, good out. Bad in, bad out. Does that make sense?"

"Yeah."

"So Jeff, let's pretend you decide you are going to stop brushing your teeth for one month. What would happen to your teeth?"

"Well, they would get dirty, my breath would smell, I'd probably start getting toothaches and have to go to the dentist."

"And you probably wouldn't have a girl friend either, right?"

He laughs and gets a big smile on his face and says, "right".

"So, Jeff, would that be a good decision or a bad one?"

"A bad one."

I begin to snap my fingers as I say, "Okay, now how long does it take to change your mind and do something different?"

He immediately gets the idea and says, "not very long".

"That's right! In fact, your brain has already made that decision faster than I can snap my fingers together. So, after going without brushing your teeth for one month could you change the effects of not brushing your teeth?"

"Sure, I just start brushing again."

"How long would it take to change the effects of not brushing your teeth?"

"Oh, probably a week or two, maybe longer."

"That's right, but it always begins with making a different choice, right?"

"Right."

So, from what you've heard so far, does this all make sense?"

"Yeah, it does."

In the next phase of the interview I structure the questions in such a way as to not allow Jeff the opportunity to express a victim mentality. A person expressing this type of attitude places blame on everyone and everything for their current situation.

"Now Jeff, let's see how this principle or law is working in your life right now, okay?

"Okay."

"Tell me again, what is happening with you right now. Remember, I really don't care about what has happened in your past, because your past does not equal your future. Let's make a list on the chalkboard of all the things that are going on at school and at home right now."

Jeff goes into deep thought and pauses after each response. It appears that he is seriously sorting out what is really happening in his life right now.

"Right now I'm not getting along with my parents."

"So, Jeff, tell me in what ways you are not clicking with your parents."

"Well, they don't trust me, I feel like they are constantly on my case, they want to know about everything I'm doing, I feel like I'm a prisoner in my own home. We just can't talk to each other without getting into arguments and they keep threatening to ground me for every little thing."

"Boy Jeff, from what you've just expressed, it sounds like everyone at home is not too happy with life."

"You can say that again!"

"Okay, how about at school?"

"My attendance is bad."

"So what kind of problems does that cause?"

"Well, I'm failing all my classes, my P.O. (Probation Officer) is threatening to throw me in juvenile hall, and they want to kick me out of school."

"Okay, so who's in control of your choices right now?"

"Well, I guess I am."

"Right, these consequences you're getting, are they good or bad?"

"Well, they're not very good."

"Jeff, do you like feeling happy or sad?"

"Well, I like feeling happy."

"So, with the choices you're making, do you feel happy or sad?"

"Not too happy I guess."

"Again Jeff, who's in control of your choices?"

"I guess I am."

"That's exactly right! I have no power over your choices and you have no power over the choices I make. You have no power over your parent's decisions and they have no power over your decisions. You have total control over every decision you make for every situation. The effects you get are a direct result of the choices you make. In fact, you make thousands of decisions every day without consciously realizing you're doing it. You must do something different to get different results in your life. I've found that if someone really wants something different for his life and he continues to do the same things over and over, nothing will ever change. So, in order to change the consequences we must choose to do something different. Does that make sense?"

"Yeah."

"Now, what can you do, right now, in order to have different consequences in your life?"

"Well, if I do the opposite of what I am doing right now, I guess things would change."

"Right, because going to school, studying, and being prepared for class will be the things that all successful students do. Jeff, let's imagine that you and I get into a time machine and we travel 10 years into the future. How old will you be?"

"Well, let's see, I'd be around 24."

"Now imagine what you would like to be doing with your life. Tell me what you think you would like to be doing."

"I'd like to be a teacher."

"Wow, that's great! Why do you want to be a teacher?"

"Because, I want to be able to help kids just like me."

"Man, that's awesome Jeff. What are some of the good benefits of being a teacher?"

"Good salary, vacation time and great benefits."

"What kind of car would you like to be driving."

"A really nice car."

26

"What would you like for your house to look like."

"A nice house with three or four bedrooms."

"Okay Jeff, let's get back into our time machine and head back to the present. Now that we're back let me ask you a very important question. Is what you're doing right now going to help you get the things you want like being a teacher, having a nice car and a nice house?"

"No!"

"So, what will it take for you to reach your goal of having a good job and all the other nice things you'd like to have?"

"Well, I guess I'll have to make better choices."

"Why?"

"If I don't, things will never change."

"Let me ask you another extremely important question before we conclude this session. Have you already made a decision to go for your dream goal? Remember, I am looking for students that want to do something different, accept responsibility for their lives, and practice making new decisions and choices that will give them the happiness they are looking for. So, be completely honest with me Jeff, because if you are not honest with me, you are not being honest with yourself. And being honest with yourself is the most important gift we can give ourselves."

"Yeah, I want to do that."

At this point in our bonding experience it is extremely important to get a strong commitment from Jeff.

"So, from what you learned about the greatest mental law of the universe, the law of cause and effect, you are telling me that you are willing to make a shift in your thinking, to begin working together to create the future you desire."

At this point Jeff will either say yes and really mean it or say yes and try to manipulate me by telling me what he thinks I want to hear. I carefully watch his non verbal communication to see how truthful he is being with me. Regardless of what I think his intent is, I then reach across the table and take his hand firmly and warmly in my right hand and cover his hand with my left.

"Jeff, I want you to know that I am making a commitment to give you my best everyday. The only way our handshake will be nullified is if you decide to make choices and decisions inconsistent with what you tell me you really want. My next question Jeff, is how will I know that you are making better choices and decisions?"

"Probably by what I'm doing in class."

"Please be more specific. What exactly would you be doing?"

"You know, coming to school, being on time, doing my homework. I would also get along with the other kids in school."

"Great. I think you really understand what you need to do to have a better future for yourself. I must tell you that it is your choice as to whether you stay in my class or not. I know you have the intelligence and ability to be excellent this year. You have all the resources you need. Working together we will be able to accomplish some great things. Not only will I be the teacher and you will be learning from me, but you will also be a teacher because I plan to learn some things from you. It will be a win/win situation for both of us."

The shift in Jeff's thinking is very evident. Some of these kids will say they have bought in, but they are only giving lip service to what they know I want to hear. It doesn't take long for their true beliefs to become evident. Even though, by their continued poor choices, it is evident that they have not made that shift, the seed for change has, none the less, been planted and may take many years to grow and influence their lives. It is essential that we as a society realize that this type of approach brings out the best in people and we need to be consistent in our approach whether or not they understand what we are endeavoring to do. Their time with you may be the only time they feel that someone really cares about them. Consistency in following through with the consequences of their actions lets them know that you do care. The time you spend with them will be given to helping them understand that the better choices they make, the more pleasurable the results of those choices. This needs to be done in a calm and kind way that says if I didn't care, I would let you do whatever you please. There's one thing you can count on and take to the bank, kids don't care how much you know, until they know how much you care!

ACTION PLAN

1

EXPECTATIONS

"An expectation is an idea, belief or agreement someone entertains in their mind. The choices one makes concerning behaviors is based on this premise."

During the interview with Jeff, I let him know what my expectations were at the very beginning. This allowed him to know specifically why we were in that situation and what the outcome would be. Expectations, when communicated properly are very powerful tools for helping anyone make choices. An expectation is an idea, belief or agreement someone entertains in their mind. The choices one makes concerning behaviors is based on this premise.

At different points throughout the interview with Jeff I gave him the following expectations:

"The next 30 minutes you will be spending with me will be quite different from anything you have previously experienced."

"I am looking for young people who are really wanting to do something different."

"By the end of this session you will be completely honest with me and let me know if this program is what you're looking for."

"You have control over the consequences in your life through the decisions you make in every situation."

I have discovered that young people will move to the level of expectations that others have of them, whether it is positive or negative. Teenagers brought up in a negative environment where they are expected to be bad, will be bad. How many times have we heard adults say to children, "you're a bad, bad boy" or "you just can't do anything right, can you?" or "you are so lazy". Children want to please us and they will try their best to live up to our expectations of them. When we make these kind of statements, they will do their best to live up to what they perceive regarding these expectations. On the other hand, teenagers brought up in an environment where they are surrounded by positive expectations such as: "What you did was not acceptable, I still love you and I know that in the future you will make a better decision" or "I know that was a difficult task and you did the best you could. I know with practice you will continue to do even better", will automatically do their best to live up to those expectations.

In order to help teenagers like Jeff desire new choices and behaviors, the authority figures in their world must give them empowering expectations by what they say and do. All young people, when you really take the time to listen, will tell you they want to be happy and have a good life. Just because they are labeled "at-risk", "troubled" or "unhappy" by society, does not mean they are bad. They just haven't been taught the strategies of making good choices. Many of them are extremely intelligent, but because they have been told over and over again that they are bad, losers, lazy, stupid just to name a few negative expectations that have been placed on them, they hate life and school and see no value in the educational experiences being offered to them.

The story is told about an adolescent girl who had a desire to be an artist. The people in her life convinced her that she must be a wife, mother, grandmother and help her husband on their farm. She gave in to their expectations and for over 60 years she lived according to their expectations. Then, after her husband passed away, her family doctor told her she would have to give up farming. It was at this time in her life when she was in her late 70's that she finally took up her love of painting. She went to the store, bought the needed supplies, and began painting. Within a few years this woman's great gift and talent had been recognized by artists all over the world. In fact, just one of her paintings sold for more money than she and her husband had earned the entire time they worked the farm. Grandma Moses became one of the most celebrated artists of her time and an icon in American history.

When anyone working with a teenager wonders what they can do to help them, it is absolutely essential that they point them in the direction for achieving their inner potential and dreams. When you really believe that every human being has untapped potential and you understand your role in that relationship, magical things can happen.

In Jeff's case, his new choices and decisions began to immediately give him a greater sense of being in control of his own destiny. He chose to come to school, do his work, work at getting along with the other students and participate in class. Jeff's image of school and his image of himself began to change. He would come in early before class to just sit and talk about the things that mattered most to him. He began to smile more, laugh a lot and he appeared to be enjoying himself. His mom contacted me and let me know he had really hated school the last three or four years, but now he was excited about attending and being in my class.

It makes no difference whether young people find themselves in school, juvenile hall, youth authority, boot camp, etc., when they meet someone who believes in them and has high expectations for them, a magical transition can begin to take place. What we desperately need are more people who know how to spread this kind of magic wherever they go.

There is one important thing you need to remember. It is crucial that these young people receive constant support and encouragement from someone who has a genuine concern for their future. This is needed to negate all of the negative programming they have had for most of their lives.

ACTION PLAN

2

TOUCH

"At the end of the interview, not only did I shake his hand, but when I took his hand in my right hand I covered his hand with my left. I let him know, in no uncertain terms, that the only way this handshake would be nullified was if he decided to make choices inconsistent with what he tells me he really wants. I let him know that I will not be the one to open my hands and let him go. He will be the one who pulls his hand away by the decisions he makes."

One of the most valuable ways of establishing contact with any human being is through the medium of touch. Today many individuals that work with young people have been influenced by the hysteria that surrounds the media's reports on abuse or inappropriate touching. Because of this many people tend to steer away from any form of touching. However, touch is an integral part of our domestication as a human being. In fact, touch is one of the most important areas of activities for our own personal and emotional development. If this need is not met in appropriate ways by significant adults, it is likely that many of our youth will turn to violence, drugs and pre-marital sex to meet this need.

Learning how important it is for a human being to receive validation through touch is an eye opener for many people who work with children and youth. Some people believe it is enough just to say they care. When working with a young person of any age it is imperative that we understand they do have a need to be touched in a positive way. We must also understand, because of previous conditioning experiences, touching them may not be appropriate in the initial stages of forming and developing a relationship. One must be tuned into a young person's need to the level at which they feel comfortable with touch. By watching a person's body language you are given an instant message as to whether or not they are comfortable with an initial hand shake. If they seem to hesitate or move away then you must wait until you have established a trust relationship to make that physical contact.

If you'll remember, at the initial point of contact with Jeff, I deliberately gave him a very energetic welcome, a warm caring smile and a handshake. I wanted to let him know I was really excited about meeting him and getting to know him personally. In most situations when a young person is called into a meeting, they usually anticipate the worst. In their eyes, some authority figure they have never met is going to give them a stern lecture about all their problems and in no uncertain terms warn them that they better get their lives together or else.

In most cases, these young people will not refuse your initial handshake. They may be reticent and their handshake maybe very wishy-washy but most of the time they will shake your hand. If by chance they do reject your handshake, there is no need to panic. At the end of the interview, if done properly and you convey the message that you really care, they will welcome your handshake.

At the end of the interview, not only did I shake his hand, but when I took his hand in my right hand I covered his hand with my left. I let him know, in no uncertain terms, that the only way this handshake would be nullified was if he decided to make choices inconsistent with what he tells me he really wants. I let him know that I will not be the one to open my hands and let him go. He will be the one who pulls his hand away by the decisions he makes.

All of us have been traumatized to some degree and these young people are no different. As time progresses in the development of your relationship you may find that he will actually seek you out for the touch he needs. When you start validating teenagers through touch, as well as really paying attention to their non-verbal communications, you will notice in time a tremendous change in their attitude toward you and also how they feel about themselves. It is truly a miracle taking place right in front of your eyes. The exciting thing is that this miracle can be repeated over and over again by using this principle every day.

When working with young people in any capacity, learning to take a small amount of time to reinforce the power of touch is crucial. Greeting them with a handshake, putting your hand on their shoulder, patting them on the back or putting your arm around their shoulder are examples of very fast and appropriate ways of communicating to someone that you care. Young people will go from a point of no touching whatsoever to a daily expression of needing to be touched in positive ways. Some young boys find it hard to express themselves verbally or even physically through the normal means of touch. They will however let you know you're okay by brushing against you in a playful way, pretending to punch you in the arm or stomach, giving you a high-five or making contact with you when you're involved in some type of physical exercise or game.

In the game of basketball for instance, the game naturally allows for physical contact. It is okay to grab and hold someone in a game situation. Apart from the game, most young people would be very uncomfortable in giving you a hug and therefore tend to express how they feel about you by establishing contact in non-threatening situations. When you are invited to participate in a contact sport, it is usually a sign that you are a quality person in their life. They are needing and wanting to be closer to you. Take the opportunity to understand what their behavior is really saying.

Many times the girls, as well as the boys, will want to participate in a contact sport. But when the girls have been abused either sexually or physically, you will find that it is difficult for them to experience any form of touch. They may bump against your arm or allow you to pat them on the back but one thing for sure they will let you know when you have over stepped the boundary. Just be sensitive to their needs and when they know they can fully trust you, you will know that a pat on the back or an arm around the shoulder is a welcome form of touch from someone they know really cares about them as a whole person.

When I was working with these young people in the classroom, I would meet them at the door when they arrived in the morning. I would shake hands with each student, welcome them to the class and let them know this was going to be a great day. If by chance a student did not want to shake hands, I just smiled and gave them the same expectation I gave the others. It was usually not long before they came around and would start shaking my hand. At the end of the class time, I would stand at the door and shake hands with each student that left and tell them to enjoy the rest of the day and that

I was looking forward to seeing them tomorrow.

At times, I would be busy at my desk when the bell would ring to end the school session and if I didn't get to the door, the students would line up at the door and yell at me to get over there to shake their hands so they could leave. What an experience to see these "troubled teenagers" begging for that quality touch, affirmations and expectations. This was probably the highlight of my day. What a delight, being able to see the change in these young people in such a short amount of time.

ACTION PLAN

3

AFFIRMATIONS

"Along with the powerful, positive, emotional attachment to the words we use, it is equally important to use positive reinforcement or verbal compliments for behaviors that you want to see repeated."

W ithout a doubt, the use of words or affirmations in our daily language is a very powerful way to move people to action. Words can be positive and empowering or negative and humiliating. Unfortunately many times children get labeled with very negative nicknames that can stay with them throughout their lives. These words evoke strong negative emotional states which may lead them to perform destructive behaviors.

On the other hand, language can be used in a very positive way. The words we choose to use should have a strong, positive emotional tone attached to them. An example would be some of the expressions I used when talking with Jeff, such as:

"Jeff, I am really glad to meet you, I have really been looking forward to this meeting."

"Jeff, thank you for being honest with me about everything."

"Right, I knew you were pretty smart."

"Wow, that's great! Why do you want to be a teacher?"

"I know you have the intelligence and ability to be excellent this year."

Another example of using positive emotional words is by saying "good morning". The emotional tone attached to these two simple words will give us a deep and immediate insight into the mind set of that individual. This really gives us a clue as to whether this person is having a good day, is depressed, sad, excited, having fun, being distracted, etc. I have made it a practice over the last five years to say good morning to everyone I meet. I have done this thousands of times. When I use these words I say it with lots of enthusiasm and with a big smile on my face. Try this yourself. It is extremely interesting to observe the reactions of people. The individuals responding to your "good morning" will let you know by their response how they have chosen to think about their own personal day. After a lengthy period of time when you use this approach you'll find a lot of people begin to reciprocate. I love to see this happen. It means they now value what you have been doing. There is a definite shift in their thinking that allows them to respond to your interaction with them. This specific change in thinking is called a paradigm shift. When a paradigm shift takes place it lets you know the individual has changed the "meaning" of their experience in relationship to you. Instead of "good morning" being just another trite, mundane, repetitious response, it becomes one of true significance for the user. In their mind you have become a significant person in their world. They have a new picture in their mind of a positive relationship with an adult.

Along with the powerful, positive, emotional attachment to the words we use, it is equally important to use verbal compliments for behaviors that you want to see repeated. Verbal compliments should always be used when anyone demonstrates a positive action that benefits themselves or someone else. Too often people are looking for the things people do wrong instead of what they are doing well.

An example in Jeff's case would be when in a specific situation he would have completed an assignment of his own on time or helped someone else who was having a difficult time, I would reinforce his behavior by saying the following:

"Jeff, thank you for working to complete this assignment so quickly, keep up the good work. I love it when you demonstrate your ability to get the job done."

"Jeff, I really appreciate the way you helped Barbara with today's assignment. She was struggling and having a difficult time and you showed a lot of concern and patience in helping her complete the assignment."

A study was conducted in a kindergarten classroom with children five to six years of age. For the first part of the school year the teacher set up the expectations that everyone was to only say and do good things toward each member of the class. This teacher was careful to reinforce the student's positive behavior. For weeks the students lived up to the new guidelines as set forth by their teacher. The number of negative incidents from this class was very negligible. Then sometime later the teacher, instead of reinforcing the good behaviors of her students, began to ignore them. What do you think happened? Well, as you probably guessed, the behavior of the students declined dramatically. Instead of helping each other and being concerned about each other's well being, they became highly competitive, turning to negative and acting out behaviors. The number of incidents referred to the principal skyrocketed. When the teacher returned to her earlier teaching style of positive reinforcement and regard for each student in her class, the behavior returned to a warm and caring atmosphere.

A former Disney executive, that I had the pleasure of meeting, reported that during their staff meetings and planning sessions if anyone on the team brought up anything that was negative to the accomplishment of their brainstorming, that individual would be required to put money in the pot to pay for lunch. He made a point to say their staff meetings took on a wonderful and exciting air of positive anticipation. This approach kept everyone thinking with the creative or right side of their brains instead of being constantly analytical and picking things apart and trying to find reasons why something would not work.

The point is clear. We should use positive reinforcement when the situation calls for it. Giving someone positive, complimentary feedback when they have chosen a good behavior will strengthen the likelihood of that behavior being repeated. When we notice good things people do and reinforce that behavior they really feel good about themselves. This increases their self esteem. They begin to feel like someone with value and worth.

Before I close this chapter dealing with positive affirmations, I would like to bring to your attention words I call "explosive" words. They are words like "never", "always", "nobody", "everybody", etc. Some examples used by the young people we work with are: "you never let me do anything", "you always yell at me", "nobody cares about me", "everybody hates me". They way to deal with these "explosive" words is to ask the individual to be more specific. "Who specifically is nobody?" "Has there ever been a time when I have not yelled at you?" At the same time we as the significant adult in their lives must remember that when we use these same words they can be very destructive. For example: "You never do anything right!" "Why do I always have to remind you?" "Everybody else finished, why not you?" Even though these statements might be true, they evoke a very volatile response in most people. Some alternative questions or statements might be, "I noticed you are having trouble finishing. What can I do to help?" "What can we do to help you remember the things you need to do?" When you start using these phrases, you will establish an immediate rapport and as you continue in this manner you will have these young people "eating out of your hand".

On the other hand, these teenagers will, for the most part, try your patience. When you observe them making a poor decision and you must confront them, it is crucial that you do it in a way that is pleasant for all concerned. As one of my mentors, Dr. William Glasser taught me, "Before reacting, ask yourself this question: Is what I'm about to say or do going to move me closer or further away in my relationship with this person?"

An example might be:

I always gave my students time in class to complete their assignments. Because of the environment they entered into when they left my classroom, I knew that the chances of them getting anything done was pretty slim. I was there to see that they succeeded and not to put undue pressure on them. When I would see them reading a book that didn't relate to the class, I would walk to their seat and very quietly and calmly let them know that I was really excited that they enjoyed reading. My concern was that I had given them time in the classroom to finish their work and they could either finish it now or continue reading and stay after school to finish the assignment. It was their choice. I **never** reprimanded them in a negative way. Punishment must never enter into the picture. These young people need all the support and positive affirmations they can get. When there is a very extreme situation where they are making really poor choices, it is our responsibility as adults and role models to take care of the situation in a positive way.

In my five years while working with these students and using the approach that I have explained in this book, I rarely had a situation where there were any verbal confrontations among the students. However, in my subsequent research, study, and experience, I have found a system that works in dealing with most conflicts. Because of time constraints in the classroom I have simplified a process developed by Ron and Roxanne Claassen in a publication entitled "Making Things Right".

An example might be:

Two students start yelling and screaming and using extreme profanity toward each other in the classroom. I tell them to sit on opposite sides of the room and I will talk with them in just a moment. Next I ask the class to work on an assignment or talk quietly in their seats while I talk to each party for a few minutes.

While talking with each individual, I would ask them to describe what just took place from their perception. I would also ask them how they feel right now. Then I would ask them to recall the discussion we had about personal responsibility before school began to ascertain what they remember about making good choices. Based on their response I would then guide them using good leading questions, such as: "Whose behavior can you control?" "Was the choice you made in class today effective or ineffective?" This way each student is forced to think about the fact that they were responsible for their personal actions in this incident. They will not be allowed to play the victim role.

Then I present them with two choices: 1) to agree to meet with me and the other student to resolve this situation through a conflict resolution process or 2) write the other person a letter of apology. Because of the choices presented, either choice will hopefully lead to an improved relationship.

When you meet with each student individually and they agree to meet to resolve this conflict, then you would give each of them the guidelines of the mediation process that will be followed.

1. As the teacher I will lead the meeting.
2. You are allowed to let me know if you feel the meeting is not fair.
3. There will be no name calling or interrupting.
4. Be as honest as you can.
5. Agree to summarize what you hear.

When each student agrees with the process you set a time and place that works for everyone. This needs to take place as soon as possible after the incident. The location should be neutral to all parties ie: another classroom, office, etc. The time should be convenient with very little chance of interruption, preferably before or after school when other students and staff are not present.

When you meet with both parties together you need to review the guidelines and I have found that the following outline works in most situations.

First, with the parties present, establish the resolution ground rules and ask for agreement from both parties:

- Allow me to lead the meeting
- Let me know if you feel the meeting is not fair
- There will be no name calling or interrupting
- Be as honest as you can
- Agree to summarize

Next, to define the problem from each person's perspective decide who will speak first, then follow the guidelines below:

- Ask Person 1 to describe what happened-facts
- Ask Person 2 to summarize
- Ask Person 1 to describe their feelings
- Ask Person 2 to summarize

- Ask Person 2 to describe what happened-facts
- Ask Person 1 to summarize
- Ask Person 2 to describe their feelings
- Ask Person 1 to summarize

Ask both students to:

1. Make a list of ways to make things as right as possible, have them be very specific!
2. Alternating between lists, have each student share their list. Put their suggestions on a visible sheet of paper.
3. Evaluate the options and decide which ones will make things as right as possible.
4. Clarify future intentions if a similar situation were to arise again.

Ask each student the following questions:

1. Is this agreement reasonable and respectful for both of you?
2. Will this agreement solve this problem and future problems if kept?

We all have an innate desire to please people. Young people, who never seem to be able to please the adults around them, will do almost anything for a relationship with someone who values them as a human being and will fulfill those desires.

Reminder for all of us:

Trust grows when agreements are made and kept

-Ron and Roxanne Claassen

ACTION PLAN

4

CHOICES

&

CONSEQUENCES

"I am what I am and I am where I am because of all the cumulative choices I have made over the years. I have discovered that if something in my life is not the way I want it to be, then I, and I alone must choose to do something different to get different results."

I t has taken me a long time to come to the realization that I have no power or control over the decisions and choices people make. Having grown up in an environment influenced by external control, I was trapped in my thinking that what was right for me had to be right for everyone else. Putting pressure on people, making someone feel guilty, or threatening them with retribution has become the method of choice for most people in our world. Fortunately, by focusing on my own personal growth, I have come to the realization that I am only responsible for myself and the decisions I make. I am what I am and I am where I am because of all the cumulative choices I have made over the years. I have discovered that if something in my life is not the way I want it to be, then I, and I alone must choose to do something different to get different results.

.When I was talking with Jeff, I was able to help him discover the reality of the principle we call "cause and effect" and the power it has to affect our lives. Jeff was able to make the connection between his choices and the consequences he was experiencing. He came to the realization that he was the one who was in control over what was going on in his world.

Learning to make good choices is a skill that can be learned. By practicing this skill, we empower ourselves to create our own destiny. From the time we begin to learn how to use our primary language, we naturally encounter situations where we have many opportunities to exercise our decision making. Unfortunately, most of the adults in our world feel that children do not have the capacity to make good decisions because they are not mature or do not have enough experiences in life. This carries over to their teenage years when most people are still telling them what to do. According to Dr. William Glasser, the need for having power in one's life is as much an inherent need as the need for food, shelter, air, freedom, love and acceptance. Without opportunities to exercise the decision making process and either reaping the rewards of that decision or suffering the consequences, they never gain a sense of power over their own lives. One thing you can be sure of is that the need for power must be filled. By turning to smoking, drugs, alcohol, sex, truancy, anorexia, bulimia, etc. they are able to sense that power. The problem is they have never been allowed to make choices and suffer the consequences of poor choices. They are so starved for the ability to have power over their own lives that they don't realize that the consequences they are about to experience will have some very damaging affects in their lives. Before they realize what has happened, their lives are in a tailspin that is very difficult to reverse.

The best situation of course is to allow children to make choices and then either praise them for the best choice or allow them to suffer the consequences of a poor choice. Your child may come and ask you to take him to his friend's house because it is cold outside and he does not want to ride his bike. You have company coming that evening and you need to vacuum the carpet. You do not have enough time to do both so you tell your child that if he will vacuum the carpet, then you will have time to take him to his friend's house. It is his choice and he can either help you so you will have time to take him or he can bundle up and ride his bike. It doesn't matter which choice he makes, what matters is that he will decide for himself whether or not the choice he made was a good choice or a poor choice The more choices children are allowed to make, the quicker they will be able to evaluate the situation and learn to make the best choice. By forcing them to do either one task or the other takes away their power and their ability to learn from their poor choices. Then, when confronted with peer pressure, they have not had the experience of making intelligent decisions with results that will be in their best interest.

When teenagers have not had the privilege of learning the benefit of making good choices at an early age, the poor decisions they have made are creating extreme difficulties and keeping them from becoming a responsible adult. It then becomes our responsibility to teach them these decision making processes. We must give them choices and allow them to suffer the consequences. The key to accomplishing this successfully is to let them know that we really care about them. As I stated at the end of The Guided Tour, "they don't care how much you know until they know how much you care".

The following is an example of how we can help students with their decision making process. While working in the classroom you realize that one of the students, let's say Jeff, is not participating in a group project. You take him aside and let him know that it is important that everyone participate. You realize that maybe this is not a good day for him and he may have a lot of other things on his mind so you are giving him the choice to either participate cooperatively with the rest of the students or he can go to the principal's office and sit quietly and think about the things that are bothering him. If he chooses to go to the principal's office, I explain that when I have a chance I will come and get him and if he wants, we can talk about what is bothering him. If he chooses to stay in class and then does not participate I would take him aside and let him know that he has made his decision, by not participating, to go to the principal's office. Whatever happens in this situation, it was Jeff's choice that put him in whatever situation he finds himself. He can either stay with his friends and participate or spend time alone in the principal's office. It is important for teenagers to learn in a safe environment that they do have power and they can make their own choices. By having someone guide those choices, they can learn that with good choices come happy outcomes and with poor choices come consequences that are sometimes less pleasant than the good choice they could have made. This scenario can be duplicated anywhere. This type of training should be going on in our homes, on the job, in husband-wife relationships and on sports teams. Teaching young people how to be empowered by choice is an exciting way to change behaviors for generations to come.

ACTION PLAN

5

COMMUNICATION

"It is imperative that an adult steps up to the plate and takes an interest in these young people. They are looking for someone to listen to them and they will take anyone who is available."

C ommunication is more than just talking with someone. According to the American Heritage Dictionary, communication is the art and technique of using words effectively to impart information or ideas.

In this interview I want to make sure there are no communication barriers. I want Jeff to be very specific and be aware that I am not guessing at what he means. He is not wondering if I understood him or if I was reading things into what he said. When he told me that his elementary school years were "okay", some of the questions I asked, to help him be more specific, were:

"Jeff, could you give me more specific information like what your grades were like?"

"So Jeff, tell me, how did you get along with your teachers and classmates in elementary school?"

Another important element of this interview was to summarize each portion of our time together. When we finished discussing his elementary school experience, I repeated back to him what I understood him to say about those years of his life.

"So, from what you've told me so far, we could say that your elementary school years were happy ones, you got pretty good grades and you got along with your teachers and classmates? Is that correct?

Since I get an affirmative answer to this question, we can go on and discuss another important segment of his life. His years in middle school. Because we are breaking his life down piece by piece, we can see where the breakdown started. What I have found most of the time, is that the breakdown occurs when these students enter the seventh and eighth grades. If they have not established a good strong relationship and an open line of communication with a significant adult, they will establish strong relationships with peers who are going through the same confusion and insecurities. It is imperative that an adult steps up to the plate and takes an interest in these young people. They are looking for someone to listen to them and they will take anyone who is available.

By taking the time to really understand what these young people are saying and making sure that they know you understand, will, more times than not, begin to establish a trusting relationship in that short amount of time you spend together. But this is the easy part. When they accept you into their world and believe that you are sincere, it is crucial that you hold up your end of the bargain. They have had so many disappointments in life and they need to know they can trust you. The lines of communication must be kept open. There can be no guessing at what they mean. Being specific and summarizing what they have shared with you, takes away all the guess work.

ACTION PLAN

6

LEARNING STYLES

It is fascinating to observe young people when they are in situations where they are truly having fun and learning something new at the same time.

In the preceding chapter on communication we learned how to be very specific when communicating with young people. Another aspect of communication and probably one of the most important is to understand that when working with anyone, whether a child, teenager, or adult, the fact is that human beings all have unique, but specific ways they process and retrieve information.

It is fascinating to observe young people when they are in situations where they are truly having fun and learning something new at the same time. Unfortunately, in many of our schools, teachers and leaders either assume all of their students learn the same way or they just have no idea period.

There are basically three (3) types of learners: visual, auditory, or kinesthetic (tactile).

Visual Learners:

A visual learner usually likes studying charts, maps, filmstrips, notes, videos, and flash cards. They usually practice visualizing or picturing words or concepts in their heads. And they also write out everything for frequent and quick visual review.

Example: I am a very visual person and I usually take volumes of notes when I'm taking a class, getting directions from someone, making a shopping list for the grocery store, etc. I have a very good visual recall of people's faces and can remember someone's face, even when I haven't seen them in many years.

Auditory Learners:

This second type of learner usually doesn't take a lot of notes on paper, but they do inside their head. To recall the information they will also talk with themselves out loud or quietly. Auditory people, after reading something, typically have a great ability to recall the information and recite back to others the main points of the information they processed.

Example: My wife Mary, being auditory, can read a rather long piece of text and very easily and quite naturally, although not necessarily verbatim, repeat the information back to me with such ease, you would think she wrote the material, whether it be a joke or a funny story.

Kinesthetic (Tactile) Learners:

The third type of learner loves to write things down, trace information on paper, doodle, and keep volumes of lecture notes. They also like to make study sheets and associate class materials with real-world things or occurrences. Typically these types of learners have a very high need to move in very rhythmic ways.

Example: Kinesthetic individuals can be observed performing a rocking motion in a very straight-backed chair, tapping their feet on the floor, tapping their fingers on the tops of their desks, playing with coins in their pockets, or other movements that are unique to themselves.

This type of information is extremely significant for parents, teachers, employers, or anyone who is working with other people. We can never assume that everyone learns the same way. When asked questions about how they enjoy learning new things, most people can tell you how they like to learn, although they may not know how to define the process or processes as we have described above. It is also significant to know that we all use the three styles at different times, but we typically use one or two of these styles on a regular basis.

There are very simple ways to detect what learning style is most dominate in each individual. In the following chapter we will outline the specific patterns of eye movements and verbal predicates people use to process information.

ACTION PLAN

7

DETECTING
LEARNING
STYLES

*Our learning styles are predetermined
by our personal individual genetics.*

Our learning styles are predetermined by our individual genetics. All human beings operate in three main learning modalities: Visual, Auditory or Kinesthetic. Each individual has a lead modality. To ascertain which one the person you are working with generally utilitzes, you can observe the specific locations and directions the eyes move when asked different types of questions. Past and present information is catalogued in the brain. When retreiving information the eyes will indicate which modality is being used.

In the following examples, you will learn how a visual person retreives pictures from their recent and distant past and how they create new pictures when asked for information they have never seen before. This creates an excellent way of determining whether a person is being truthful or not. When retriveing information auditorially you will learn the positioning of their eyes as they are listening for sounds and dialogue from their past or creating new sounds. You will learn how a kinesthetic person reconnects with their emotions and experiences to recall past and present information and also how they create a new sensation.

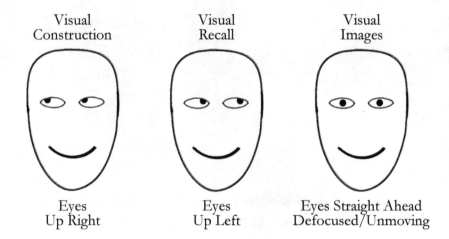

Visual
Construction

Visual
Recall

Visual
Images

Eyes
Up Right

Eyes
Up Left

Eyes Straight Ahead
Defocused/Unmoving

Visual Construction

Seeing images of things that were never seen before or seeing things differently than they were seen before. Questions that usually elicit this kind of processing include:

"What would an orange Hippopotamus with purple spots look like?"

"What would you look like from the other side of the room?"

Visual Recall

Seeing images of things seen before in their distant past. Sample questions that usually elicit this kind of processing include:

"What did the first house you remember living in look like?"

"What was the color of your first bicycle/car?"

Visual Image

Seeing images of things seen before in their more recent past. Sample questions that usually elicit this kind of processing include:

"What color is your car?"

"What does your favorite dress/shirt look like?"

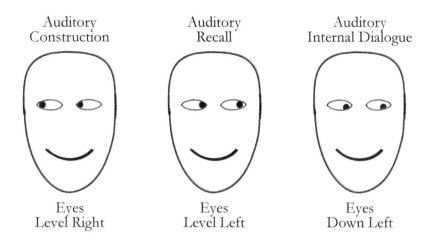

Auditory construction
Hearing sounds not heard before. Questions that tend to elicit this kind of processing include:

"What would the sound of clapping turning into the sound of birds singing sound like?"

"What would your name sound like backwards?"

Auditory recall
Remembering sounds heard before. Questions that usually elicit this kind of processing include:
"What's the last thing I said?"
"What does your alarm clock sound like?"

Auditory dialogue
Talking to oneself. Questions that tend to elicit this kind of processing include:
"Say something to yourself that you often say to yourself."
"Recite the Pledge of Allegiance."

Physical/Emotional
Feelings

Eyes
Down Right

Kinesthetic

Feeling emotions, tactile sensations (sense of touch), or proprio-
ceptive feelings (feelings of muscle movement). Questions to elicit
this kind of processing include:
"What does it feel like to be happy?"
"What is the feeling of touching a pine cone?"
"What does it feel like to run?"

An additional way to detect which modality a person is operating
out of is to listen to the predicates they are using in their speech.
To communicate effectively and let a person know that you are
truly interested in what they are saying you need to become skilled
at using predicates that match the processing style the individual
is using at the time. The meaning that you want to get across to
the person is "I understand you". The following is an example of
what you might say to each individual to match their processing
style:

Meaning	I understand you
Visual	That <u>looks</u> good to me.
Auditory	I <u>hear</u> what you are saying
Kinesthetic	That <u>feels</u> right to me.

An example of other predicates is as follows:

Visual Predicate	Auditory Predicates	Kinesthetic Predicates
Look	Listen	Feel
Glance	In tune with	Get in touch
Show	Rings a bell	Grab
Picture	Loud	Grasp

As you practice and become proficient in understanding and putting into use these skills, you will find that the rapport you build will allow you to connect with each person you come in contact with in a powerful way. It is a powerful tool that once mastered will become so natural you won't even have to consciously think about it. Remember, practice makes permanent.

PERSONAL

CHALLENGE

"We must break the cycle for these children and young people and if you change the life of just one person you will have started a whole new chain of events."

W e have been working with young people since we were teenagers ourselves. The one reoccurring theme we have seen over the years is that we have many unhappy teenagers in our world today. Not only are they unhappy, but they have no connection with a significant adult who really cares and will take the time to listen and teach them about life, communication, touching, expectations, affirmations, choices and consequences. Not only are they unhappy teenagers, but they grow up to be unhappy adults. Not only unhappy, but angry, hurt and neglected. I have heard many people say, "Well, that's the parents responsibility" and that has always been true. But our over-crowded juvenile halls, jails and prisons are letting us know that someone is letting these young people slip through the system.

Many of you will say, "What difference can I make". "There are so many and I am just one person". If each person will reach just one child or teenager and become that one significant adult in their lives, wouldn't it be worth it? We must break the cycle for these children and young people and if you change the life of just one person you will have started a whole new chain of events. On the grander scale we may not live long enough to experience the full impact our actions have made in the world, but I believe that if every teacher in our educational system, every parole officer, every sheriffs officer, every person who works with our young people in one way or another would take one individual and meet the needs that have been missing for so long, our world would change and our grandchildren and our great grandchildren would have a different world in which to live.

If you have read this entire book and have reached this last chapter, you are probably a person who has a heart for the young people in our society. I challenge you to take these principles, find a mentor for yourself and become a mentor to others and we can work together to help turn the tide of our society as we know it today.

EPILOGUE

When I decided to take the position of the head of the OCA (On Campus Academics) department, I was warned that I would be lucky if on any given day I had fifty percent of my students in class. Well, I took this on as a challenge.

I developed the interviewing system that you have just read about. Not only did I have a ninety percent turnout for my classes on any given day, but I had students who were failing all their classes now getting straight A's. Students who were only attending school ten percent of the time were now attending ninety percent of the time. Most of them were on time and ready to work. I made sure that I was in the classroom at least thirty minutes before class started because some of the students would come early and just sit and talk with me. It was a time when they could just chat about what they were doing with no one to correct or condemn them. This was a time of bonding with these young people. Some of them would even bring their friends in to meet me.

The success did not stop in the classroom. Some of these students would come back and visit after leaving my class to let me know how they were doing. I had teachers stop me in the halls and tell me how pleased they were with the progress of students that had previously been in my class. One teacher came to me and gave me a story one of their students had written. The assignment was to write about someone who had had a major impact on their life. One of my previous students wrote a beautiful story about his time in my classroom and how the time spent there had changed the course of his life.

Then there is the story of a young man who after the interview process came around the table and gave me a big hug. He said, "Thank you Mr. Morse, but I won't be coming to your class. I know what I need to do to get back on the right track". I never saw that young man again. I am convinced that he is doing great things in his life.

I am not sharing these experiences to brag about what I have done. I want to let you know that when you are genuinely concerned about young people and take them through a similar process that I have outlined in this book, they will know whether or not they are ready to buy into your program. Here are some of the things that are really crucial to cover when meeting with them:

1. Let them know what you expect. Be very specific.

2. Make sure you use appropriate touch whenever possible

without invading their space.

3. Give positive affirmations whenever you notice them doing anything positive. Discreetly approach them when their behavior is negative and give them the choice of continuing the behavior and suffering the consequences or changing their behavior so they can experience the rewards that come with that decision. Make sure you let them know that it is their choice.

4. Be instrumental in assisting them in understanding that the choices they made have brought them to where they are today. The choices they make today will determine their future. They are in control and have the power to change the course of their lives.

5. Help them to understand the law of "Cause and Effect". Every choice they make will have a consequence. Just like gravity. What goes up must come down.

6. Communicate effectively. Make sure you are very specific and help them to be specific. It is important that you understand each other clearly.

It would be great if each of these young people would change the course of their lives and graduate at the top of their class. However, we only have these young people for a very short time in their lives. We can be assured that everything we say and do is recorded in their own personal computer and hopefully someday, somewhere, something will happen that will remind them of what we have been able to share with them. The one thing we must remember is that if we only affect one life, it will be worth the effort. When these young people act on the information they have received and share it with others, they will begin breaking cycles one by one.

Two years ago I left the classroom setting and many people ask me why I left when I was being so successful. As I listened to other teachers, I could sense the frustration they were feeling toward their profession and students. When there was a shortage of substitutes I would fill in for other classes during my prep period. When I met that teacher in the hall after his return he would apologize for his class and say how sorry he was that I had to deal with these "disrespectful kids". I let him know that it was a privilege to fill in for him and that I thought he had a great group of young people.

You see, I just used these same steps I have given you. I met them at the door with a handshake and welcomed them to the class. I was enthusiastic. I let them know what my expectations were for the hour we would spend together. I led the class with all the enthusiasm I could muster. I was in control and they were captivated. They left with smiles on their faces and a quickness in their step. It was always fun and a challenge to step into these classrooms.

I left because I felt that I could teach others to do what I do. I was affecting the lives of fifteen to twenty young people a year. How many more young people could I affect if I could teach others to do what I was doing.

So wherever you are, I challenge you to make a difference. Choose to do something different and reap the rewards that come from seeing these young people turn the corner and look forward to a brighter future.

If you are ready to accept this challenge, please send me an e-mail and let me know. I will be more than happy to assist you in any way I can.

STUDENT COMMENTS

I would like to share some of the comments I have received from students who have completed my classes. They have experienced the same interviewing process I have shared with you. This will give you an idea of the impact you can have on young people when you give them the power to make their own choices backed by a true respect and unconditional regard for their future.

This first student wrote the following paper as a requirement for an English teacher the year after he was in my class. The teacher thought I would be interested in the overall affect I was having on my students.

(The OCA that is mentioned is the title of the program - On Campus Academics).

Student #1

When people hear OCA they think of ditchers, drug addicts and kids that don't have a future. But Mr. Morse changed all that. He listened to his students and heard what they had to say. Then he helped them with their problems and how to solve them. He did not care why they were there. He saw right thru that and looked inside of them and saw their real selves. Mr. Morse stayed with them when other teachers would have given up on them. This way he earned their respect.

When most students enter OCA they enter with bad grades or bad attitudes. They think they are all alone in the world and that no one knows what they have gone through. But, Mr. Morse has heard it all. He used to be a probation officer, so if he doesn't understand no one will. When teachers put students into OCA they think it's over for them. They think once you enter OCA you will probably drop out a few weeks later. OCA used to be a place where you just dropped "no chance" kids. The kids of OCA could not have a break with the rest of the regular students in school or go to the rallies for the sports teams. When Mr. Morse became the teacher he fought for us so we could have the breaks and attend the rallies.

Most of all, he made us work hard and helped us start making good grades. Of course, each student had to be willing to try, not all did. Before I entered OCA I had never gotten an A before, in my whole life. Mr. Morse taught me I didn't get A's because I never tried. He was right!

Sometimes, when I think about it, I realize it was a good thing I got in trouble and was sent to the OCA class, because if I hadn't

I would never have met Mr. Morse. Mr. Morse has helped change me and my friends life for the better. For that we will always be grateful and he will always have our respect.

The remaining comments were from students who where attending my class. I asked for feedback about what they had learned during the year.

Student #2

I have been taught this year that I have the power to do things if I put my mind to it. If I fail I can start over, that the past doesn't matter. It's how I can change for the future. And no matter what people say its how I feel and about what I want for myself! When I grow up I want to be like you and teach kids how to use their minds also. Some changes I have made in myself are that everyone fails but all you have to do is try again and not put anyone else down for failing.

Students #3

I think I have changed from the beginning of the year because before I didn't think of the consequences and didn't do my work because I thought I couldn't do it. But now I feel like I'm smart enough to do anything. I see my future in a world of success. I think I have a great future ahead of me.

Student #4

Before I came to your class I choose not to do my work because if my parents and my teacher didn't care why should I. Then I came to your class. I started doing my work because you told me that my parents and my teacher can't get me to where I want to go. That it was all up to me. And I also made a change in me. Now I have more confidence and I believe that I can be anything I want if I put my mind to it.

Student #5

My mind is my own. I will control it. I have the power. Those three sentences mean a lot to me. They really made me think of the control we have of decisions. I also learned how to be strong through peer pressure and how to handle situations. The changes I've made is in my attitude. My attitude has changed a lot towards school. My sense of direction towards what to do and what not to do. I see my future the way I plan it. My way because, "my mind is my own".

Student #6

I think I did alright this year in here. I learned a lot about making right choices. I have done more of my work than I did last year. I have been not bad about my attendance. I think I'll do better in the future.

Student #7

I have been successful this year in my attendance of school and my academic expectations of myself have changed greatly this school year. While attending this class I have realized that I'm better than I thought I was I'm not like I was in a sense that I won't settle for my life the way it is now. I mean I've improved, sure, but I would do better. In Junior High I went maybe half the time I was suppose to and my GPA was probably a 1.5. Now it's like a 3.5 because I have mostly A's and one B. Next year I will apply what Mr. Morse taught me this year and pull a straight 4.0 and get a job and on top of all that do something I haven't done in years and get perfect attendance.

AUTHORS' NOTE

All our adult lives we have worked as employees in one arena or another. It was always secure and the thought of working for ourselves never entered our minds. We were so focused on helping other people that we never really had time to discover the possibilities that existed for us. While beginning to focus more on our own personal growth, we came across Brian Tracy's materials that really seemed to express what we believed but never took time to really concentrate on applying to our own lives. As we listened to his tapes, studied his material and were able to meet Brian and become an affiliate in his organization, we began to realize that there were possibilities we never dreamed of waiting for us. We realized that we had the potential of taking our message and spreading it around the world. We also realized that we had to step out of our comfort zone to accomplish this task. We know that the time that we spent with Brian through his tapes and other materials were extremely instrumental in our own personal growth.

Below you will find a list of some of Brian's material that really changed our thinking about how we could have an affect all over the world.

Tracy, Brian, *"The Science of Self-Confidence"* An audio tape series
Tracy, Brian, *"Thinking Big"* An audio tape series

While utilizing the internet to research other individuals whose ideas paralleled Jon's, we came across Dr. William Glasser. We were really excited when we realized how extensive his work is in the area of choice theory. It was so similar to the strategies Jon had been using we knew we must meet this person, who like ourselves, had a tremendous desire to see young people in our world succeed.

Even before we met Dr. Glasser, Jon began studying his work and found that we shared many of the same ideas. While this process you have read about is Jon's own creation, we have been able to extract even more information and encouragement from Dr. Glasser and his wife Carleen.

Following you will find a bibliography of a few of their books that we believe you will find helpful in your search to find a better way of dealing with the young people you come in contact with on a daily basis.

Glasser, W., M.D. (1998), *The Quality School: Managing Students Without Coercion.*

Glasser, W., M.D. (1998), *Choice Theory: A New Psychology of Personal Freedom.*

Glasser, Carleen, M.Ed. (1998), *The Quality World Activity Series*

Glasser, W., M.D. (2000), *Every Student Can Succeed*

Glasser, W., M.D. (2000), *Counseling with Choice Theory*

Glasser, W., M.D. (2002), *Unhappy Teenagers*

These and other books are available through the William Glasser Institute in Los Angeles, California (800) 899-0688

CPSIA information can be obtained
at www.ICGtesting.com
Printed in the USA
LVHW031419010323
740660LV00001B/69